THE SHADOW OWNER'S COMPANION

Eleanor Hooker

DEDALUS PRESS
DUBLIN, IRELAND

ACKNOWLEDGEMENTS

Acknowledgements are due to the editors of the following where a number of these poems originally appeared: *Agenda* (UK), *The SHOp, Crannóg, The Stinging Fly, WOW! Anthology, Wordlegs* and *Leave Us Some Unreality: New Writing from the Oscar Wilde Centre, Trinity College Dublin.*

Warm thanks to Pat Boran for his editorial guidance, kindness and laughter. Thanks to Gerald Dawe, Deirdre Madden, Carlo Gébler, Molly McCloskey and Jonathan Williams for their encouragement and direction on the MPhil in Creative Writing at Trinity College, Dublin.

Thanks to my friend Pat Kelly for his quip that one should 'stay going'.

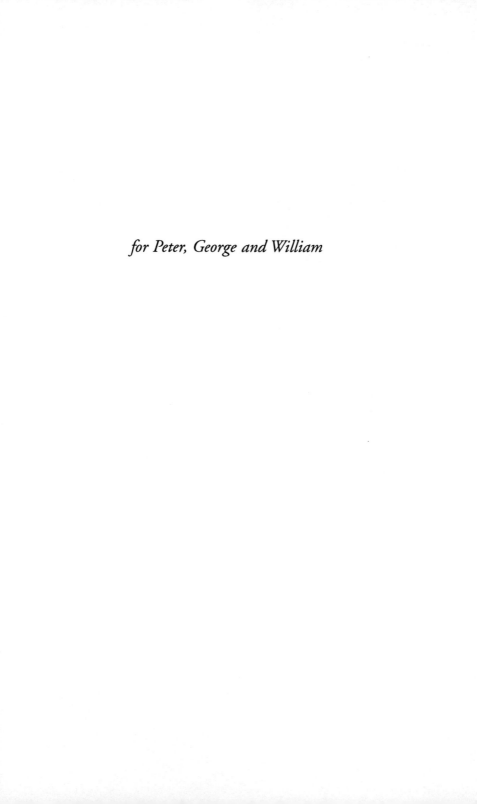

for Peter, George and William

Contents

My guardian angel is afraid of the dark. He pretends he's not, sends me ahead, tells me he'll be along in a moment.

—Charles Simic, 'The World Doesn't End'

Three Things

Three things I keep secure: my life, my truth, my boys.
As I contemplate the surface of the lake,
Three things I long to lose: my doubts, my fears, their lies.

And so I dive. Through underwater gloom, pike eyes
Find me, their torn mouths lipstick-stained. Make no mistake,
Three things I keep secure: my life, my truth, my boys.

Four times, four times ago, pike bit through my cries, dyed
My heart ink-black, hands fish-scaled, tattooed till I ached
To lose three things at last: my doubts, my fears, their lies.

I cannot keep or lose it all, nor mollify
The pike, whose teeth grow from clenched fists. For their sake,
These things I've kept secure: my life, my truth, my boys,

For even when they're dead, razor-toothed pike will try
To swallow whole, attempt to gut their prey, to rake
Through things I long to lose: my doubts, my fears, their lies.

Lock it down inside ink-stains, sketch it inside joy,
So when the pike swims close, he'll never ever take
Three things I've kept secure: my life, my truth, my boys,
Just things I long to lose: my doubts, my fears, their lies.

The Island

So humid, even the wooden bannisters sweat.
Out on the island, woodpeckers head-butt Alder trees,
Like shocked heartbeats, the rapid *lub-dub lub-dub*

Will find its echo in me. My dog laps water,
Making delicious sounds, delicious thirst-quenching sounds.
Her tongue hangs long, quivering, stretched to tear.

"Close your mouth," I say, as I launch *Kibihee.* The boathouse
    is cool,
Air soothed in sponged light. *Kibihee's* timbers sigh against the
    blue
Tickle of water. In this summer heat as I oar us out of depth

The shoreline shimmers unsteadily and when the engine coughs
We are underway at last. The island's trees are lined with birds,
Heraldic wings outstretched drying in the sun,

A cormorant arboretum. They choir a deep, harsh croak,
A cacophony of dissent at our approach. But they know well
We will not be turned; we mean to find a way onto the island.

I cut the motor and on the breeze *Kibihee* drifts closer
To the rocky shore. The movement of swans in ballet
Overhead is like a warning sign.

Another summer I would have left, but not today.
Though more and more birds arrive, today I hold my nerve.
One by one cormorants come to greet me, landing on the
    gunwale,

Their backward-forward toes gripping *Kibihee*. This is what
I've waited for, my 'come-true story' and one I've heard every
	summer
Of my life from my Granddad. Lifted from the water,

My boat protests her age. Alarmed by the creaking of her planks,
I shift my weight as we are settled quite steady, in the steady
	quiet
Of a summer oak, deep, deep within the island,

A hidden place, where looking would not find me.
"For how long?" Sasha asks. Inside this island dogs talk
and cormorants know the limit of fear.

This is where trees walk to the water's edge
To watch sailors fumble with the wind and bow at trees
On the opposite shore, rooted there forever.

"For just today," I say. To the arrhythmic drumbeat from my
	heart,
We are rocked asleep inside a dream of *Kibihee* being rocked
	asleep
Inside a dream. And, when I awake, I'll know it's time.

Cell Phone

for Peter

I cup your voice to my ear.
Your warming breath against my skin,
You hold my hand though you're not here.

You tell me not to let my fears
Stalk every step back to my kin,
To cup your voice to my ear.

This narrowed world is wheezed with tears
As stove-hat ghouls stick dolls with pins.
You hold my hand though you're not here.

Cut, emptied hearts lean in and jeer
At dancing headless mannequins.
I cup your voice to my ear

And tell you how the night's laid bare
As though the world is pulsed with sin;
You hold my hand though you're not here.

I reach my goal—no longer care
That watchmen bar the hallowed inn.
I cup your voice to my ear;
You hold my hand though you're not here.

Fishing

One, two, three four five,
Once I caught a little fish alive.

It had three urns in its belly,
Inside of each an ash tree grew,
One had Granddad's face on its trunk,
Another had Old Grandpa's hands in its branches,
The third had Old Granny's smile in its roots.

Six, seven, eight nine ten,
I had to let it go again.

It had three eyes, unusual for any fish:
One eye saw the world beneath the water,
The second looked, but never saw,
The third had a mercury-filled cataract
That told the future in filigree pictures.

Why did you let it go?

I let it go because it was a pike,
I know that now, and know too
That pike will find their own way home.
And look, it bit my finger so.

Which finger did it bite?

The little finger on the right.
It choked, *this will stop you telling*, and then it smiled.
I let it go, because I have always known my way home,
And have learned to breathe beneath the water.

Prelude

It has the soft raw edge of an open wound.
I touch the keys and the music holds me earth-bound.
Along the passage a rustle of silk as the shadows whistle,
And the room sighs as the dead return.

Chrysalis

Locked down for over
forty years. Ugly grub.
Doubting ever an emergence
from that state.

Each segment a two-footed
dance, toe tapped to the
lashings from the larch.
Lock down and hide!

The pike sent her to
the shark. The essay
scored in pupils' blood
to be read aloud to

fifth and sixth and seventh.
Her story surely funny as
they threw their heads
and screamed and screamed

with glee. Her sisters in the
second row, sat side by side.
Mary cried and Margaret smiled
and she smiled back but that

was wrong, and she was beaten
for the smile and the unfunny
story and the laughing stopped.
Lock down and hide!

Haiku

Twinkling stars up high,
Are they very pointy?
Wonder of my child.

Read us a story,
a story from your head, Mum,
make it full of us.

I can't marry you,
I've met a girl I love loads.
From my son aged four.

William, where are you?
In Saint Peter's Square, I scream.
Found, I hold him tight.

The ghost is back, Mum,
I can't breathe when she is near.
Make her go away.

Cold Snap

I loved it when the world went white.
The land was hushed and ghost-like.
Constellations pierced the night light,
And, deep in the lake, the still pike ...

The land was hushed and ghost-like.
A greedy moon ate up the sky,
Constellations pierced the night light,
The anaemic sun was mystified.

A greedy moon ate up the sky,
Repeating portions of the day,
The anaemic sun was mystified,
Spiders web-wove ice-spun crochet.

Repeating portions of the day,
Constellations pierced the night light,
Spiders web-wove ice-spun crochet,
I loved it when the world went white.

Wasted Time

In every room a ticking clock, hickory-dickory.
None that tell the time, though each one measures lasting
     mysteries,
The fall and fall of ruptured moments, unfulfilled
     prehistories.

Glow Stone

for George

Hurtling past moon-day's unmade fields, past all
Those wasted hours further back the same train.
Getting up to find you, a stricken trawl
Through storybook days, damped with fretful rain.
The same train, but your car grappled back to
Yesterday. I managed just to ravel
Time as it spliced my need to nurture you.
How could I let this happen and travel
Down the same lines as my parents?
Listen to me, child; this is not the worst.
Please allow a moment for atonement.
We'll snatch a piece of nevermore, but first,
Entrust me with that glow-stone love, to creel
For night the light of day, a moon-day's steal.

Nightmare

A cobalt night in blue relief
and the hunt begins.
The green grass black
and the talking baby frightens me.
Bug-eyed horrors hover in
our shadows, lingering, carnivorous.
Wailing now to let him stay,
He stumbles after, the talking baby.

Drop under the yickety-yackety
picket fence. A treacherous fork
in the road. I know well the dangers.
Where I go the baby follows. I urge him
back to the black-green grass, behind the
yickety-yackety picket fence.
"You'll be safer there," I promise.

He crawls back under with pleas
to follow. We neither saw the pit
that he fell in, in velvet silence. A
small hand held the edge but
slipped away beneath my grip.
A cobalt night in blue relief
and the hunt begins.

The Fall

Oh she bared her soul alright; it fell from a star cloud
Reigned by *Canis Major*. They knew it was authentic,
It whimpered like an unknown set loose inside a crowd
Of urban predators: fierce curs and savage sceptics
That roamed in packs. A few select gave shelter in
The telling, clad the naked soul in their protection,
Made suspect bargains to house her in a harlequin
that, masked and silenced, looked like her, even wore her skin.
But being undressed is like an honest thought, it cannot
Lie with dogs; it is the thing in itself, nothing more.
The truth is beastly but does not wag the tale. No, that
Is the subplot tellers invent when they call her *whore*.
And though her flesh is marked by canines, they strain to blame
Her first fall, judging original sin her true shame.

Breathing Lessons

Can you breathe better now?

... as she sucks all the air from your lungs
and binds you in her purple vice of demands.

Hold still, let me drive this rusty nail through
Your breast, scratch a hex on your heart.

Can you breathe better now?

You don't need this arm, it's greedy, selfish
Of you to want two. Let me twist it off.

Let me saw you in half, you were never
Whole anyway. See how I help you, doll?

Can you breathe better now?

Afternoon Tea

Afternoon tea, four p.m. in her lair. Polish, gilt, flair, all illusion.
Decay reeking on her breath, the air besmirched by her rot.
Inclined, to better view her clawed feet, she strains the tea
Through your deaf ear. A drip-drop, drip-drop drumming
Through your skull. You look away but catch her eye double
Blinking in your hand. Roll it to and fro. Used pike
Teeth form her iris, her reflections sneer and mock you.
Wrung out, she mops a spill with your freshly
Laundered beating heart. Her brew is
Full of lies, made yours now too;
It was sifted through your life,
Remember? Time to go.
"A photograph before you leave, my dear,"
Your soul snapped … and framed … and hung.

Granddad

for Dad

And especially when red angels lit
From his pipe and set his chest aglow
With rubies, did I love my Granddad,
In the holiest clothes in all the land.

When Hamlet's spectre flickered
At the edges, and bleak school rain
Thrashed our house, and Granddad
Spelled *sure* when asked for *shur*

And I didn't correct for the love of him.
When Mother and sister breathed
"Nell! He's gone," and Granddad still—
Beside me, and brother sketched

Him on old brown paper, till Granddad
Lunged a green-filled cough at those
Who thought he'd gone and almost
Measured. When stories of Kerry

And the Hunger and the Troubles
Made of him a giant, *illness* shrunk
Him back. And when at last he left
His tales behind, he was the first dead

I'd ever seen. I longed to lift
That yellow sunken, unsmiling face
To find the man who whispered
Faith faith, when red angels set

His chest aglow with rubies.

Lost

In my dream we moved house.
Worry scurried inside my chest
catching my breath, rasping my throat.
I couldn't remember, couldn't remember

our old address where I was certain
an exquisite something was left behind.
In my dream I dreamt I'd journeyed there
to find the house adrift, room from room.

On a hanger in an empty wardrobe hung a
severed memory. Found all my old thoughts,
neatly folded and colour-coded, the black ones at
the back faded gray. In my dream I dreamt

I cried and cried, certain an exquisite
something was left behind and I couldn't
remember, couldn't remember the name
for it. I wasn't really there at all, the mirrors

would not reflect me, so I ceased to dream
of that other place and opened my eyes. Here around
exquisite somethings, I no longer see, no longer feel.
Dreams untying dreams.

Someone Tell Me

Have you ever found yourself,
having flown safely, suddenly, contrarily,
transported to the front seat of your brother's
car, all your childhood selves crying
on the back seat, demanding attention,
while the car is out of control, ice-skidding
down and around unspoken grief.

Have you?

Have you ever noticed how the embossed
paper, walled in the sick room, is a living, moving,
breathing thing that absorbs all thought,
night-time, blood, ash trees, old oaks,
firsts, lasts, the moon, a parent? How the days
of your life are written on those walls, how this day
fails to be a blue-lit, sun-skied place?

Well have you?

Have you ever then found yourself
huddled with your brothers and sisters
in a vaulted doorway, watching sepia imageries
roll down the street, pulling the sea from your eyes,
but still any talk of your father's illness fills
the space with a falling down, skidding
out-of-control, orphaned childhood panic?

Well have you? I need you to tell me. Please.

Birthday Greetings

My right ear pressed to the track, feeling for trains,
it began to rain frogs. They fell like globs of green
ugliness on the side of my head. So many fell, I could
no longer tell if my train or croaking frogs pulsed the track.
One that landed in my hair belched a greeting, and, lying there
with my right ear pressed to the railway track, I apologized to him.
Frogs are not globs of green ugliness: jealousy is and spite too,
    mean-toothed
talk is, campaigns of hate and making children feel unloved are
    most definite
types of green ugliness. The frog told me two things I'd forgotten:
my train would arrive ahead of time and that day was my birthday.

Alethiometer

for John & Fedelma Tierney

I have one marble only, glass-curled greens and blue.
It's kept inside a golden globe with turquoise studs,
I swing it from a chain: my dowsing stone, my truth-seer.
Once it knocked against an ancient head, cracked it so its walnut
    core
Leaked sepia images of a being lived inside another time, another
    age,
Before the image replaced the real and the real was more than
    shadow.

Outside the cave I glassed the play of light and shadow,
And when my only marble fell from its golden globe onto a blue
Tiled ocean floor, I swam after. The ancient head, wise with age,
Told me he had too lost his, recalled the studs
Inside the coloured orb, their curled blues, their seedy core
His own two eyes: Learian days that left him sightless and a seer.

My ancient friend dismissed the lies of a mummer seer
Whose falsest claim is that to love someone is to dispossess him of
    his shadow,
To wipe out every trace of him. Is this not indeed a murderous
    future? Our core
Belief that we are sworn to good and not extremes is not illusory.
    Those blue-
Eyed boys in ivory towers profess there is no truth, no self,
    nothings real; the studs
That breed such suasive tales are only there to fill the storybooks
    of our age.

Along the furrows of my brow I found a little pebble, it seemed
an age
Since I had lost my marble. This purple stone weighed but a
fraction of a seer.
It rattles in the golden globe, its hollow ring dislodging all the
turquoise studs.
In the desert of the real, we watched the sun expand and then
contract my shadow.
The ancient head has none. Though he is dead, we still talk.
When the moon is blue
And the sky is starry nights, we harvest all the fruits of happy
thoughts and core

Them for their seeds. "Is all of speech deception, all meaning at
its core
Inherently unsound?" I asked the wise old head. He'd reached an
age,
He said, and no longer feared such things, was satisfied there were
no blue-
Prints or master schemes, simple truths apply—it does not take a
seer
To tell you that the darkest hour is just before the dawn. All of us
are shadow-
Dancing but mustn't let the darkness intercept the light. The
mettle studs

He riveted to the heart of my resolve are turquoise studs
In reinforced solutions. I've made up two new moulds, hollowed
out their core
For curled glass in colours of the universe, whose negatives in
shadow
Graphs are images of beings lived inside another time, another
age,

Before I was madder than unreason and he mapped inscape as a
  seer
And gladness had another view, before betrayal choked intentions
  blue.

Talk on this blue-green sphere sets the lens within our glass-eye
  studs,
Through which the seer sees us stumble through the worth of
  words, in that core
Bewitchment of every age that cannot tell the real from dancing
  shadow.

Singing Ice

Across the rigid ice-scape they heave
And haul colossal cables to the shadows
On the opposite shore. We shudder at the echoing
Crack and coil of tensile steel on the cold lid of winter.

Back and forth the spectres murmur.
We hear them hum the hymns of the dead;
Ceremonial chants that rise and fall for hours,
That, gathering volume, resonate like breathless

Air across empty glass. We venture out a foot or so.
Beneath us air-sharks drop and dive through
Slivers of thickening water, then rise to slam
The frozen under-surface. They tear long rips

That roar along the night, tracking us and splitting
The marbled floor at our feet. The percussions
Petrify the living and the dead sing on.

A Whisper

I hid a whisper behind the aspen trees so
when the time was right the air might carry it home.

And when the time was right the aspen trees would tremble
with my whispered breath, and the sound would soak the clear

blue lake in a cloudless light and it would sigh, look up,
look out and know the clear blue day in a cloudless light.

Long ago you planted aspen trees behind the breeze so when
lightly stroked they moaned with quivering delight,

and, when the time was right, a murmuring rising in the air
recalled your ancient whisper placed behind the aspen trees.

Old Harry

With our bow head to wind off Old Harry,
we dropped anchor, took transits to the headland
and the lighthouse, till the anchor ploughed
the sea bed, dug in and held fast.

And the sea raged.

Crouched in the bow, I manned the anchor,
Peter took soundings off the stern, and Colin
on the helm called the numbered lengths
of rope to fairlead to the sea.

And the sea raged.

And the sea raged and heaped insult
after insult upon us. At the command to brace,
I locked the warp and brace–brace–braced,
the most offensive wave lifting me clear
and slamming me back on the deck.

And the sea raged.

But I held the line; our umbilicus to life.
With our bow head to wind we veered
back to Old Harry. Anticipating a surge
in temper every fifth, we managed
the lifeboat astern of rocks and shallows.

And the sea raged.

As we neared the cliff face, Old Harry
yawned and the sea pushed us past his jagged
teeth into his cavernous mouth, back and further
back until we saw them, could almost touch them.

And the sea raged.

Two swimmers, shallow-shelved, battered, clutching
wet walls. Cold. We could see their fear, carried
on their backs, urging them to jump as we urged
them to stay put, to hold on. Echo. Echo. Echo.

And outside the sea raged.

And, inside Old Harry, the sea thought she had
all my lines, but a sheet bend to another warp
allowed the four more feet required. Two swimmers
jumped on board and we swaddled them in warmth.

And outside the sea raged.

Two of us in bow now. Tugging, hauling, coiling
furiously on the line, pulling, springing ourselves
back to sea, back to our anchor, back to safety,
away from Old Harry and his craggy hungry mouth.

And the sea raged.

We weighed anchor and turned and ran from harm.
Colin stayed atop the highest wave, stealing from
one to the next, feathering the throttle as the sea
tried to take us, bow over stern, down, down, down
to win back her prize.

Recovery

He's overdue, that's all we know.
As the lifeboat tugs the reigns of snow-
blown steeds, crew take each new wave
on a rising trot. The rhythmic pitch

of our engine's blades is the sound
of hope in tortured air. Overhead
the sky lies low with blame, seeking
solace in the speckled mirror of the lake.

We search the run and flow of current
winds, racing points on our compass.
Very soon we find his skiff, holed
and broken by the gales. And then,

close by, we find him too. Drowned.
Alone and still. We stop and bow our heads,
all silent now, even the wind has stilled its
ragged wail. But this is no Ophelian scene,

there are no fragrant flowers here, February
insists on monochromes of brown and ash,
with wintered reeds and lough his only cradle.
Gone is colour from this life. Gray lake

infused, a waxen absence dyes his face
and hands. His eyes. We break our gaze
as overboard into this other scene we slide,
to gather up, tender to the last of rites.

Lough Derg

Veiled by the ancients for her celestial beauty,
banished by the Gods for her voracious
passions … They took her breath and named
it wind, drove her to the underworld
so all remained upon the earth, her flowing

curls that lick and lap the furls of time.
Mute, and still she waits. Her locks a lake that
all would enter, penetrate for their pleasure.
Wordless struggles every day. The wind's attempt
to give her voice draws back her head
to kiss her mouth. A tempest in the making.

Now, squalls get tangled in her hair and wisps pulled free
lash my face as thunder rumbles overhead. Oaks bend
and beeches break and the howling is the sound
of unnamed fears as sail is preyed upon, fearful
of the blackening falling skies. A numbing,

wrenching gale draws back a final time, revealing
reddened eyes, the bloodied face of aged beauty.
Balefully she regards me. Snatching gulpings
from my throat, the gusts exhale it in her mouth;
a tormented wail rebukes me for my lack of faith.

54

Rain clouds unfurl, fumble on the Clare shore, low set
to the water. Checking the line our crew calls 'Squall',
counting down as breathy patches darken on the surface,

warning signs as we harden up to weather. And then it's
upon us. 54 heels and we sit up, hang out, and take
all the lifts we can. On port tack with no rights, 45

charges up on starboard. Whispers, 'We'll dip below her'.
I ease the sheet as you bear away, and with a hair's breadth
our timbers almost kiss, six feet visible only beneath their

boom. Before the mark slips back in time we tack onto
starboard. A giant gust retches across our bow and the
shrouds wail. A low moaning, a keening for the wind

vibrates through the forward thwart, along the gunwale,
varies its pitch with every flurry. Our tell-tales—wool from
Granny's sweater—say we're pinching, so we ease the pain.

Round the mark onto a run, a lolling death roll, so we slight
a drop of plate and sheet in. Balanced now, 54 surges into
a steady sprint and crosses the finish, panting, upright and intact.

Boat Builder

Jimmy's hands made our boats. Like wood themselves,
aged tools scored by time and gnarled by bone.
Hands that glean from wood its soul can shelve
the clinkered planks to keel, form the backbone
of the craft with the delicacy of
a surgeon grafting vessels to a heart.
A shy man, building boats his one true love,
none but God could part him from his art.
There's no apprentice learning at his side,
so when Jimmy does run out of life we
will sail remembrances of him. Untied
from all concerns, he says he'll moor up at this quay,
de-rig his boat and heave his anchor to the sky.
Then evermore from land he'll watch his fleet sail by.

The Clowns

Seven. I was seven when I went to
see the circus first. I have
hated them ever since.

Pitiless clowns hauled a
widow from her seat. She wore
a scarf and old black clothes,

and cried in knee-length
bloomers when they tore her
skirt. I cried too. Granny wore

pink bloomers just like those.
Her blouse undid as well and
everybody laughed except me

and the old lady. Daddy said
to worry not; she was just a
clown herself and not a lady even.

It was the meanest thing he
ever said. Anyone could tell
that she was shamed.

Lazarus

The sea is different, obvious stuff—salt, higher waves,
deeper troughs, and that green, constant even when it's
heaving. Unlike a saltless lake, unlike the fleeting
colours, the hourly seasons, unlike land, port and starboard.

The whole of existence is in the water,
moving with the rapids. No one is panicking,
except me. I get sluiced off and you save me,
Holding back the dam, you save me from drowning.

I tell you what I saw, it helps that I can tell you
what I saw. I saw him push the mower, manage
just three steps and have to sit. Arms reposing
by his side, head slumped. My father dying, I think.

And I'm headlong back in the water, caught in the
rapids, the dam about to give, to drag me down in its
ungovernable flow. Those secret silent tears I wept
when I was small, so when the time would come

I would be strong for all. *Just a prelude,* the child
within whispers to my heart. I had a fight with him
at Christmas, the first I ever started, and something
broke between us. The pernicious slackening in his marrow

is draining him of life, and I cannot stop the tide that
will bear him away. We silence fear with current
chatter, we stow our dread and play at normal.
Oh Dad, don't slip your moorings, don't put out to sea just yet.

Melting Ice

The lake froze, froze all the way to
Clare, a fine bone china plate whose
glaze cracked when the melt came.

An ice block floated to our pier,
had my name scratched clearly
on its surface, had winter-words

encased inside, like seedlings
ripening for a phrase or theme.
I dragged it up the slip and left it

on the grass. Over hoar-frost days
and Baltic nights—snowshoes,
Jack Frost, goose bumps and laughter,

the Northern Lights, snowfields,
thistledown, arctic bears, ice marbles,
and more, so much more,
emerged from the melting ice.

Songs of the Sea

At Kilmore town, ancient carols are sung;
Legends say the sea will drown their town.
Casting stones into the sea is wrong.
Storm-crested waves drag silent sail down.

Legends say the sea will drown their town,
a silver coin beneath the mast brings luck,
storm-crested waves drag silent sail down,
church bells sound when sinking ships are struck.

A silver coin beneath the mast brings luck.
True to say, what the sea wants, it gets.
Church bells sound when sinking ships are struck.
A curlew's flight makes fair-wind sailors fret.

True to say, what the sea wants, it gets.
Casting stones into the sea is wrong.
A curlew's flight makes fair-wind sailors fret.
At Kilmore town, ancient carols are sung.

Discovering a Dead Poet

A surgeon at the hospital gave me
a collection of yours; store of diamonds,
ancient gems in new settings, all are
beautifully cut. Unadorned, I try on
your utter lack of affectation, your brutal
honesty and I glitter in the dark. But
they are your jewels not mine
—neither a borrower nor a lender be—
I envy you your dæmon though,
a bird I think and from every flock.
Efficient. Ever present. Your anguish
is its carrion. Are you the wren
in the oak? I have only demons lurking
in the murky depths, razor-toothed preying
fish. I kill them everyday, don't fret.

Echoes

Made a phone call to myself today.
Called collect, thought I needed
Cheering up, hadn't spoken to a
Soul all week. I was very rude,
Don't appreciate the interruption,
or the cost. So I hung up,
That surprised me, auld bitch.
That's the last time I'll go
Out my way for me again.

Out of my way again,
That's the last time I'll go.
She surprised me, auld bitch.
So I hung up. Didn't appreciate
The interruption or the cost.
All soulless week I was very rude.
Cheering up that I hadn't spoken to a
Call collect who thought I needed
To make a phone call to myself today.

Learning to speak without a tongue

A living poet leaned against the counter
of my dreams, arms folded across his chest.
"Watch this," he said, and from every room
he summoned all my childhood selves,
and they came running through every
door. "This is how we do it," he said.
I watched in horror as my childhood
selves began to mow each other down,
bit on freckled faces, dragged themselves,
my childhood selves, down to hell. I tried
to call their names, but saw my tongue
was in his hand, which he then began to eat.

Night Watch

Sheeting rain moulds her grey hair to her skull,
her face and hands are pressed against the glass,
forked tongue feasting on hoary-winged bugs,
wild eyes darting this way and that, searching
for us inside the yellowed gloom, screeching,
screeching that she likes it, but not in the end,
not in the end, while the ninny goat eats the bark
from all the fruit trees and looks at her with his
devil eyes, as though she is the night-watchman doing his job.

Melting Lead

I've heard it all my life. Pull up
A chair inside yourself and listen.

A gland in your neck will make
your eyes pulsate, bulge with malignant staring.

Pull up a chair inside yourself and listen. Listen
to a tale of lead hands melting.

A westerly with jagged teeth snaps a beech
in two. Lead hands melt inside its hollowed core.

A fallen tree sounds the air if ears will hear
its cracking bones. Leaden hands will cannibalize

the bellied trunk for firewood. Pull up a chair
inside yourself and listen as a fractured stump

wounds the earth, and wounded earth sifts root
from shallow ground. A pyre ablaze will burn

for days, a spectral beacon at the water's edge. Lead hands
melted down to liquid silver pouring into the world,

a blister at its centre, cave bled to its heart. Pull up
a chair inside yourself and listen as your hollowed core

is filled with leaden hands, molten leaden hands
filling the empty centre at your heart.

Pull up a chair inside yourself and listen.

Wonderland

for William

Wherever I pull ivy from the land,
It rips a tear until I'm peeling back the world,
To where my cat dreams into William's hand

And your strange fear of ticking clocks stands
Over us and sessile oaks, until time unfurls
To wherever I pull ivy from the land.

Here friends unfriend, a face, a book, a brand.
So still. Their silent noise fools none. Dark doorways hurled
To where my cat dreams into William's hand

And whiskers twitch through lens with spider bands.
Deep down, beyond heaven's yards, before tether-worlds,
To wherever I pull ivy from the land,

I feast on quiet pocket-watch delight, and
Board my purring grainy train, imaged as it curls
To where my cat dreams into William's hand, and

No, you cannot come with me. You knew all this beforehand;
That I must go alone, to find that ghostly girl that twirls
To wherever I pull ivy from the land,
To where my cat dreams into William's hand.

Rejection Slips

Am I deluding myself?
Should I change my tune,
Take their word, unshelf

Myself from the noon-
Night yowl of my own voice,
Steal from the poets' spittoon

Words coughed on white?
Ghon Focus, tubercular in-voice,
O God, here I am, in the half-light,

Deluding myself.

The Shadow Owner's Companion

Solitary. She's been around for so long now, we simply
Co-exist. I know she's there. At night she rocks in the left
Corners of our bedroom, her chair held together with my fear
Of the dark. She stays there, mostly, in the dark. Sometimes,
She sleeps at the bottom of the lake. She wakes me in my dreams
And I ignore her, but then she does her special trick; hovers just
Above me, her weight not on me. I spoon up to you. 'I'm
    frightened,' I say,
'Mind me.' And you warm me not to tell. My dreams, they
    frighten
You too. I won't look at her; I know she could never be unseen,
    unheard of,
For ever and ever.

Sunset

They played too close to the edge of the world,
but it was the sun caught fire, not the stars. It threw itself
into the lake, at the back, near the sharp edge.
We watched in awe as the lake and the sky
with its rinsed clouds all caught fire too.
Blood and flames soaked the western world red,
and some in the east laughed, before the sun went out
    completely.

Walking Through the Treetops

Looking up, we discovered each and every tree-top
hugging. Hugging fiercely in a moonlit arc, a leafy,

longing, tight embrace, the length of endless skyscape.
Being a flightless grounded thing, I scrambled up the oldest oak

to wander through the tree-tops. Birds were packing summer
sounds, leaving us behind. A robin sat close by and stared

and stared, incredulous at the sheer inelegance of me, until I
looked away ashamed. *Walk here, if you will, you'll never fly.*

That same Robin took a piccolo from his chest and played:

> *Of snowless winters*
> *Of Christmas treks*
> *Of family gone*
> *Of wingless flight*
> *Of seasoned woods*
> *And walking through the treetops.*

The Oak

The old oak spoke to me
today, when I hugged him.
He stands at the bend on
the way. I hug him most days,
he never spoke before.

Not speaking to me today?
he asked. No, not small talk,
I said, I tell you all the live-
long days, the bright-moon
nights and all the gathering dusk.

No, not small talk, I said.
Bubbled tears soaked the earth.
I listen, he said, but I cannot
mend the live-long days, bright-
moon nights or gathering dusk.

He heaved a great long sigh;
it's the small portentous gifts
that will a soul complete, he said,
that's the truth you cannot hear.

We stayed in silence for nearly ever,
me and the old oak that stands at
the bend on the way. I hug him
everyday, but he never spoke again.

Why

Why so dark, so negative, about death?
you ask of what I write.

I am a loving wife, devoted mother
and yet none of this in poems?

I am all the lists, all the facets
of any woman's life. Still,

I cannot reassure you that
my words are also features

of an inner world, that won't
be tamed to play the fashion of

feathered graces. It is to
not be mannered, to not belong

to anyone, not even myself,
that I write. It is safer for us both

this way. Don't read the
words. Stop being afraid.

Teacher

I wore her diamond in my head for most of class.
Her crimson lipstick stained her backward sloping
teeth. Like a pike, I imagined, if she bit she would
swallow whole. Too bad yet for the bad row,

four banished then, desked evermore to every corner
of that oppressive meagre world. *Ciotóg*, left-handed,
sinistra. It smiled a vicious coldness as it drove its icicle in.
Such silent murders.

Calamity

Two monster crocodiles leashed
in the yard were for our supper. She
would kill them later, Mother said.
But they have people in their mouths,
But no one ever listened to me.

You could hide our shady little town
in the furrowed ridges on their
backs. Chewed up souls dangled
from their massive muscled jaws.
They smelled my fear and lunged.

Twin horrors inflamed with rage
rampaged along our faithless twisted
streets, snatched and tore and ate
the panicked townspeople. *I might die just here.*
But no one ever listened to me.

A self cannot become unseen by curling
up, remaining still, all crocodiles know this.
So I said, you cannot kill me, I have shards
of half-light in my heart. So they listened
and have yielded to my chains.

Wasps in a Tin Can

It didn't happen, though the thirteen indications were that it
    would, and often;
For the rest of forever it will be the thing that never happened.
I can hear their silence from here, wasps in a tin can.

Be careful what you wish for, you warned that day, *you've got to
    toughen
Up, girleen.* I'll bury bad news under wasp stings. I understand
Why it didn't happen, though the thirteen indications were that
    it would, and often.

And all the rest? Need, not want. Need, not want. Dad promised
    he would never leave us orphans,
Sure, like a cliff, only sentries of erosion could kill me. Funny,
    in my father's room, Absence commends
I should hear their silence from there, wasps in a tin can.

Another time something happened, it always does, that was
    the instant I discovered I could siphon
Fate, cut a slash in the top, let the sea sweep circus clowns and
    cobalt blues away, and heartened
Too, I made it happen, though the thirteen indications were
    that I would not ... that often.

And so they go, sullen oarsman, Ariel birdsong, and moon-
    drawn tempests—all sunken
By the flood. Ill-judged or not, I'm warned against my
    superstitions, counselled to amend
The call that I can hear their silence from here, wasps in a tin can.

Learning too, learning to unlearn the black roads, to draw
      the light from shades of childhood
And, like new skin, to wear my selfhood buttoned tight. I know
      well they'll never comprehend.
Though it didn't happen, the thirteen indications were that it
      would, and often,
I can hear their silence still from here, wasps in a tin can.

Borrowed Time

A borrowed fob-watch on my breast
ticks golden hours the other wife breaks.
She is beautiful but silent, always looking
to fix time, time she broke when sitting silently.

This is not my baby, but I hold him anyway.
I want so much for him to look at me, but instead he
grabs the hour hand on the golden fob-watch
pinned to my breast. He breaks the hours with his tiny hands.

The fob-watch burns through my chest and beats brokenly
beside my heart. Look into my eyes and you will see
them both, my heart and my broken borrowed time,
pieced together through a hole in my breast.

II

So you take us for a drive, two brothers and my father.
You drive from the passenger seat, facing backward.
Why is it up to me to watch the road from the back seat?
With hindsight, to tell you the 'when'? I am bad at this.

I warned you I was bad at this, you ask too much of me,
and now my borrowed timepiece is ticking wildly
with only a second-hand life, as the first wife watches
from her smile. It's going to be alright, you say.

Am I too old and scared for this? I listen to *Ave Marie*
twice, Caccini's then Schubert's, and I begin to cry.
I miss winter so very much. The music allows a little brumal
air to filter June, not fixing all the time in the world.

Wind Turbines

Four silent angels
on the mountain.
They clamber up

into the clouds,
emerge then disappear.
But I know it's heaven

moving, not them.
Three-armed angels
wave at me, a

large circular
three-hand motion,
and I wave back.

Majella always
led the way,
being the eldest.

She looks back
down at me
and at her

sisters, following.
When the other car
stopped theirs, it

broke them all
except their Dad.
I never saw my

friends again till
four white boxes,
different lengths,

passed our door,
and I cried into
Grandma's apron.

Visitors

All alone, just me, Sasha and Oscar,
but we hear it altogether,
the coughing down the hall.

Sasha leans in, trembling.
Oscar hides in the Aga and I,
I feel my heart beat faster.

A door closes, another opens, footfalls
dragging nearer. Frightened now,
I feel my breath breathe faster.

They know not what's beyond
the boundary walls, but as it's
just me and the dog, and the cat in the Aga …

Inky night spilt through the house;
I knocked the day over writing.
And the shadows, the shadows draw closer still.

I know they're there, I can hear the house
protesting. "I have to live here too,"
I shout, and hear their murmur of assent.

They shuffle back to the back of the house
and the coughing fades there too, but one darkness
lingers, trading places with my shadow.

NOTES

'54', p. 42

54 is a Shannon One Design (SOD), an 18ft clinker built wooden vessel, with one mainsail of 140 square feet and a modified Gaff Rig. She is sailed three up. SODs are sailed only on Lough Derg and Lough Ree. The boat numbers begin at 32 because that was the favourite number of the class captain of the first fleet of SODs. 54 was built in 1928 and before us was sailed by Grandmother Mary Hooker, who won many races in her. 45 was built in 1926 and is sailed by our cousins, the Sanders.

Lightning Source UK Ltd.
Milton Keynes UK
UKOW050622060312

188424UK00001B/43/P